We Knew Mary Baker Eddy

Copyright 1948 by The Christian Science Board of Directors. Used by permission.

MARY BAKER EDDY
Reproduced from a painting by Howard Chandler Christy

We Knew Mary Baker Eddy

SECOND SERIES

The Christian Science Publishing Society
Boston, Massachusetts, U.S.A.

All quotations in this book from "Science and Health with Key to the Scriptures," and from other writings, letters, and remarks of Mary Baker Eddy, are used by permission of the Trustees under the Will of Mary Baker Eddy.

© 1950 © 1967 The Christian Science Publishing Society
All rights reserved
Printed in the United States of America

Library of Congress Catalogue Card No. 43–7254

FOREWORD

The chapters of this book, like those of the earlier volume of similar title, are the work of men and women who had been associated closely with the Discoverer and Founder of Christian Science, Mary Baker Eddy, and consist of their personal recollections of her life and work.

It is inherent in Mrs. Eddy's teaching that the teaching should be practiced, and she set a high example in this respect. In her writings, she fully explains Christian Science, showing that the power manifested in the works of Christ Jesus is ever present and can be used now as he used it, in overcoming disease, fear, strife, lack, and evil of every kind, thus demonstrating man's likeness to God. In her many-sided experience, she consistently exemplified the use of this divine power on behalf of herself and others, and the present book supplies many further intimate views of her as she did this.

Three chapters of the book—those by Mr. Gale, Mrs. McKee, and Miss Stewart—were given as *addresses in The Mother Church Extension at Tuesday night meetings following Annual Meetings of The Mother Church. The other chapters are now presented for the first time, Mr. Adams' having been prepared especially for this volume, Miss Blackman's for the Archives of The Mother Church, and Mrs. Mims' being a stenographic transcription of a talk to a meeting of her pupils.*

The book is published at the request of The Christian Science Board of Directors.

CONTENTS

	PAGE
The Star in My Crown of Rejoicing — The Class of 1885 *by* C. LULU BLACKMAN	1
Our Leader as Teacher and Friend *by* FRANK WALTER GALE	20
The Call to Concord *by* GEORGE WENDELL ADAMS	28
An Intimate Picture of Our Leader's Final Class *by* SUE HARPER MIMS	35
An Interview with Mary Baker Eddy, and Other Memories *by* MARY STEWART	58
"With sandals on and staff in hand" *by* CLARA KNOX MCKEE	65

The Star in My Crown of Rejoicing— The Class of 1885
C. LULU BLACKMAN

PERSONAL contacts with our dearly loved Leader and teacher, Mary Baker Eddy, were limited, as one measures time, but they left pictures and impressions of rare beauty. Memory has not dimmed these but holds them ever clearly defined.

In order to more clearly reveal her graciousness, her compassionate helpfulness, and her marvelous response to my appeal for the light of Truth that finally led me to the relationship of teacher and student, I shall tell of the first coming of Christian Science in my life.

Young in years, yet without hope of healing, I was facing life from the standpoint of inevitable invalidism when, in 1884, a friend living in Chicago brought to my Nebraska home the story of a new method of healing, called "Metaphysical Healing." She could tell nothing about it except that no drugs were used. She was, however, firmly imbued with

We Knew Mary Baker Eddy

the assurance that it did heal where all other methods had failed. I was taken to Chicago to receive treatment from one of Mrs. Eddy's students and after two months of treatment was healed.

The day before I returned home I bought a copy of "Science and Health with Key to the Scriptures" by Mary Baker Eddy. There were no Christian Scientists with whom I might discuss this book, nor any to steady my untried footsteps of thought. Mrs. Eddy, through her book, was my only teacher.

At this time, Mrs. Eddy's personality made no appeal to me. It was wholly unknown, and my imagination was not awakened to even a consideration of what manner of woman this might be. I knew only that she was the author of "Science and Health with Key to the Scriptures" and that the time had come when it was imperative that a key of understanding be given me in order that the pages of Science and Health might be read with the assurance that there was no perversion of its actual meaning.

The Star in My Crown of Rejoicing

It was to me an indisputable fact that no one else could know the real meaning of the book so well as did the writer of the book. She stood to me as "the voice of one crying in the wilderness, Make straight the way of the Lord" (John 1:23). It was to this voice of Truth I made my direct appeal, and it was as the revelator of Truth she answered me.

Up to this point my mental steps were tentative, but they had brought me to the valley of decision. I wrote to ask admission to her class and with the characteristic frankness of youth and inexperience added, "If it is necessary for me to be a dissatisfied and miserable Christian, I am not ready for this instruction, for I am, and always have been, a very happy one."

This letter has always seemed to me my first coming to Mrs. Eddy, and I am sure it was her first knowledge of me. It was purely mental, but I seemed to know, even before her reply reached me, that we had met. As I look back, her answer to this letter seems very characteristic of her mode of thought and method of action. She wrote the

We Knew Mary Baker Eddy

letter herself. She offered no rebuke, she attempted no explanation. There was only the simple, loving message, "Come and see."

Later the details were worked out, and I was called to the class that convened September 14, 1885. This is counted, after these many years, the greatest privilege and joy of my life. In Hebrews 11:8 we read that "Abraham, when he was called to go out into a place which he should after receive for an inheritance, obeyed; and he went out, not knowing whither he went." These words fittingly explain my presence in that class, for Mrs. Eddy, with keenest insight, revealed "a city which hath foundations, whose builder and maker is God" (Hebrews 11:10).

When she entered the classroom, I saw her for the first time. Intuitively, the members of the class rose at her entrance, and remained standing until she was seated. She made her way to a slightly raised platform, turned, and faced us. She wore an imported black satin dress heavily beaded with tiny black jet beads, black satin slippers beaded,

The Star in My Crown of Rejoicing

and had on her rarely beautiful diamonds. These she spoke of in one of the later sessions. She stood before us, slight, graceful of carriage, and exquisitely beautiful. Then, still standing, she faced her class as one who knew herself to be a teacher by divine right. She was every inch the teacher. She turned to the student at the end of the first row and taking direct mental cognizance of this one, plainly knocked at the door of his thought. It was as if a question had been asked and answered, and a benediction given. Then her eyes rested on the next in order and the same recognition was made. This continued until each member of the class was included. No audible word voiced the purely mental contact.

In this class there were those who knew her and loved her—who had been previously taught by her and were trusted helpers upon whom she called. There were those who doubted and questioned, and still others who, even then in the classroom, seemed swayed by antagonism and said within themselves: "This is the heir; come, let us kill him, and the inheritance shall be our's" (Mark 12:7).

There is no question but that the mentality of the class, individual and collective, was uncovered to her. She felt its challenge, and she met it clear-eyed and undismayed. It was as though she dismissed something from her thought, separated herself from the mental contact, and then lifting her eyes in prayer, with one accord, the Lord's Prayer was spoken. The voice of the class said, "Our Father which art in heaven." As one with the class, and yet distinct from it, we heard these words in Mrs. Eddy's voice, "Our *dear* Father which art in heaven."

These were the first words I heard her speak. They were arresting, compelling. There was a lilt of joy in her voice; I had the impression of a child who was unafraid, and a subtle but clear assurance was with me that she dwelt consciously, confidently "in the secret place of the most High" (Psalm 91:1). It was not as though she had gone to the Father in prayer, but rather as though, because she was with the Father, she prayed. In days that followed

The Star in My Crown of Rejoicing

she gave us the Christian Science teachings on the subject of prayer, but this experience has remained with me as one of my most precious memories. The incident was a "living illustration," and added something that conveyed the very essence of her attitude on prayer.

After this audible repetition of the Lord's Prayer, Mrs. Eddy took her seat and the students resumed theirs. As she began to speak, many of the students opened notebooks and began to write. Instantly she said, "Put up your notebooks." I had written but one sentence and no other was ever added. There were others who refused to consider the command as final and, almost at once, covertly began again to make notes. With eagle eyes she detected the overt act and again repeated the words, "Put up your notebooks." All complied; then she resumed her teaching. A little later, one student began again surreptitiously to make notations. Stopping her discourse, Mrs. Eddy for the third time repeated the words emphatically and clearly, and never again was there an effort on the part of any to write down a thought or word that came from this great teacher. She at no time made any explanation of this requirement, but all my days I have blessed her for this ruling, because it compelled us to let the form go so that limited finite statements of Truth might not circumscribe the pinions of her thought. Her impartations transcended the medium of words. Words served only to convey her revelations. She gave both the letter and the spirit, but she took away the letter lest any should substitute it for the wine of the Spirit.

The first three days in the classroom gave overwhelming proof of Mrs. Eddy's understanding of God and her consistent acceptance of the fact that there was none beside Him. In my own experience, she seemed to have obliterated everything I had deemed substantial and actual. The word "God"—"God"—"God" was repeated over and over in my consciousness to the exclusion of all else.

Mrs. Eddy awakened us to the realization that she taught no mere theory but the practical, living Truth when she closed the third lesson with these

The Star in My Crown of Rejoicing

words: "Now go home and take your first patient." In my own estimation I was not ready to take a patient. She had taken away my Lord, and as yet I knew not the God she had revealed. It was a great relief to remember that I was a complete stranger in Boston and so could not possibly be called upon to give a treatment. Not willful disobedience but stress of circumstances would exempt me from the necessity or opportunity of taking a patient. The relief was short lived, for when I opened the door of my rooming place a member of the family was found to be very ill with erysipelas. When he saw that I was making haste to escape to my room he called to me: "If you can do anything for me, why don't you do it?"

The swift healing that followed my obedience to Mrs. Eddy's demand that I take my first patient gave me a keen insight into her characteristic faith in the power of the Word of God when applied through the Science she was giving to the world. She had arranged no details, provided no patients. She gave the command and knew God would

We Knew Mary Baker Eddy

"supply the wisdom and the occasion for a victory over evil" (Science and Health, p. 571).

The experience connected with this case of healing revealed to me something of the immensity of the work Mrs. Eddy had accomplished in her three days in the classroom. She had not taken up the question of animal magnetism but she had established for us her concept of God, and this true concept of God rescued and defended me from the devil and his adversaries in a time of such temptation as I had never before known. Suggestions taking form in words declared that I did not know enough of the Christian Science method to use it and declared that there was a power in my own mind that I could use instead. Error pleaded with me to substitute mortal mind for immortal Mind, arguing that mortal mind was my natural habitat, and that immortal Mind was too transcendental to avail.

I had been precipitated into a seeming mental realm where the supposititious forces of evil sought to establish the claim to equal or transcend the

The Star in My Crown of Rejoicing

power of God. I realized that there was a greater question here than that of mere physical healing. The decision to rely upon divine Mind alone was made, and I answered the tempter, "I will not resort to will power, even if the young man dies." Then as a ministering angel, this Scriptural verse came to me: "Put off thy shoes from off thy feet, for the place whereon thou standest is holy ground" (Exodus 3:5). I had forgotten the patient, but as I turned to leave the room I saw he was sleeping peacefully and that complete healing had taken place.

Thus Mrs. Eddy revealed herself to us through the power of the Word. She effaced the sense of her personality so completely that she thought, spoke, and acted from the standpoint of her oneness with the Father. In "Unity of Good" (p. 48), referring to God, Mrs. Eddy says: "He sustains my individuality. Nay, more—He *is* my individuality and my Life." So many statements made in her writings are illuminated by the fact that she lived the truth she spoke—lived it so simply, humbly, and completely that she proved what the Master meant when he said, "I and my Father are one" (John 10:30). In subsequent lessons, she took up the question of evil. I shall never forget Mrs. Eddy as she appeared when she turned from the contemplation of all good to the supposititious claim of evil, called devil. It was a revelation of Truth, but it was also an unconscious revelation of the price of learning Love which this woman had paid through vital experience, through the things she had suffered—because of the exaltation of God in her own consciousness. The picture of this loved teacher as she shared the hemlock cup with her half-comprehending students is word painted in this paragraph on page 48 of Science and Health: "Remembering the sweat of agony which fell in holy benediction on the grass of Gethsemane, shall the humblest or mightiest disciple murmur when he drinks from the same cup, and think, or even wish, to escape the exalting ordeal of sin's revenge on its destroyer? Truth and Love bestow few palms until the consummation of a life-work."

Perhaps the presence of one who was soon to

The Star in My Crown of Rejoicing

stand before the world as an opponent of Mrs. Eddy and a refuter of her teachings, in the effort to usurp her place as Leader, intensified the lights and shadows to this class. Silently and audibly this one sought to carry the students with her; when nearing the close of the class she became openly defiant. I saw and heard Mrs. Eddy deal with this state of consciousness. Her loving-kindness, gentle patience, and consecration of purpose, revealed her character. In "Miscellaneous Writings" (p. 254), Mrs. Eddy questions: "Should not the loving warning, the far-seeing wisdom, the gentle entreaty, the stern rebuke have been heeded, in return for all that love which brooded tireless over their tender years? for all that love that hath fed them with Truth,—even the bread that cometh down from heaven,—as the mother-bird tendeth her young in the rock-ribbed nest of the raven's callow brood!"

I count it a privilege to bear witness that "the loving warning, the far-seeing wisdom, the gentle entreaty, the stern rebuke" were not lacking. She reversed the sense of evil and made plain the meaning of David's words: "Whither shall I go from thy spirit? or whither shall I flee from thy presence? If I ascend up into heaven, thou art there: if I make my bed in hell, behold, thou art there" (Psalm 139:7, 8).

Mrs. Eddy always conveyed the impression to me that what she knew of evil had not come to her through the study of evil but through her exaltation of God.

The word "transparency" seems best to express my remembrance of Mrs. Eddy's personal appearance. I have never seen anyone with such swiftly changing expression, one who seemed so at one with the thought she presented. Sometimes she gave me the impression of having lived forever—that no years could measure her age; and again all sense of time seemed wiped out and she looked like a vision of youth. The beauty of her thought expressed in the physical illustrates her statement in Science and Health (p. 248), "Immortal Mind feeds the body with supernal freshness and fairness, supplying it with beautiful images of thought and destroying

The Star in My Crown of Rejoicing

the woes of sense which each day brings to a nearer tomb."

She characterized divine loveliness in these moments of supernal freshness, and gave proof of her statement, "Beauty is a thing of life, which dwells forever in the eternal Mind and reflects the charms of His goodness in expression, form, outline, and color" (Science and Health, p. 247). I count it a blessed experience to have seen this radiancy of Soul, this glory of immortality untouched by time.

Mrs. Eddy realized that those coming to Boston from a great distance felt a sense of disappointment that no church services were being held because of a vacation period. This might mean that some would never have the opportunity to hear her preach. Her gracious thoughtfulness on our behalf was evinced by her inviting us to meet on Sunday morning, when she would give to us her exposition of the ninety-first Psalm.

My appreciation of this has ever been an increasing one, and an added proof of her boundless giving.

We Knew Mary Baker Eddy

When we came close to the time of our parting, she exemplified mother-love to a marvelous degree. She told us plainly of the serpent sense that ever pursues the spiritual idea. There was admonition and warning and a great desire manifested *to protect* the Christ-idea from the destroying Herod thought. She quoted these words from Matthew 10:16: "Behold, I send you forth as sheep in the midst of wolves: be ye therefore wise as serpents, and harmless as doves." I remember her statement, "There are no short cuts in Christian Science," and she said, as I recall, "I have taken you up into the mount; I have showed you the promised land"—and then she added with finality, but also with infinite tenderness —"*but you will have to walk every step of the way to get there.*"

At no time had Mrs. Eddy remained in the room or given opportunity for speaking to her after she finished her lesson for the day. She invariably left the room before the students rose from their seats. The only exception to this procedure came at the close of the final lesson. Then she stepped to

The Star in My Crown of Rejoicing

the edge of the slightly raised platform and waited for each member of the class to come and say good-by. She shook hands with each one and spoke directly to each. I have no way of knowing what she said to others, but I know the message she gave me. As she held my hand she looked directly into my eyes and said, "Thou art mine, saith the Lord, and none shall pluck you from out my hand."

Only once after leaving Boston did I again see Mrs. Eddy. This was a few years later when a classmate and I went to Concord, New Hampshire. Because at that time friends and strangers alike were too insistent in their attempted invasion of her privacy, we decided to make no attempt to see her, or even to pass by her Pleasant View home.

However, when leaving Concord we walked to the railway station, and all unexpectedly we saw her carriage coming toward us. She smiled and bowed. Before we had gone many blocks the carriage again intercepted our way. This time Mrs. Eddy leaned forward, smiled, and waved her hand. It was a charming incident, a gracious greeting, and my last vision of the teacher whom I love dearly.

In my remembrance of Mrs. Eddy there is no one thing that impressed me more than the faith she had in her own words—her faith in the truth of the Science she has given to mankind. In "Miscellaneous Writings" (p. 99) Mrs. Eddy writes, "In no other one thing seemed Jesus of Nazareth more divine than in his faith in the immortality of his words." Mrs. Eddy's faith in the correctness of her interpretation of divine Science, when all the world doubted, transcended human belief, and revealed a "conscious, constant capacity to understand God" (Science and Health, p. 209). This faith on her part left a deep impression on me. It seemed to stand back of every word she spoke and to glorify her manifest sincerity.

Today countless numbers give loving recognition of the part the Discoverer and Founder of Christian Science has had in bringing them to conscious at-one-ment with God. Her identification with Truth is so fixed in my thought that no sense of absence, separation, or time touches my remembrance. She

The Star in My Crown of Rejoicing

stands as a reflection of ever-present Truth. I love her more today than I did yesterday, simply because through demonstration I understand her better. She is my teacher, and to have had the privilege of being taught by her is the star in my crown of rejoicing.

Our Leader as Teacher and Friend
FRANK WALTER GALE

ON a certain occasion our beloved Leader, Mary Baker Eddy, sent a message to a meeting of students, and one of the statements may well be applied to this gathering. It was: "You have convened only to convince yourselves of this grand verity: namely, the unity in Christian Science. Cherish steadfastly this fact. Adhere to the teachings of the Bible, Science and Health, and our Manual, and you will obey the law and gospel. Have one God and you will have no devil. Keep yourselves busy with divine Love" (The First Church of Christ, Scientist, and Miscellany, pp. 251, 252).

In 1885 my mother had been confined to her bed for over three years, and when the doctors finally said they could do no more for her, Christian Science was brought to her attention through a newspaper article which told of the healing of one through mental and spiritual means. This appealed to my mother, and she asked me to find out more

Our Leader as Teacher and Friend

about it. A practitioner was found who called to see my mother and commenced treatment. At the end of a week she was up and walking around the house, and by the end of another week was entirely well. We immediately secured a copy of "Science and Health with Key to the Scriptures" by Mary Baker Eddy, and my mother and I took up its study.

In 1887 we moved from San Francisco to San Diego, California, where my mother and I introduced Christian Science and started the healing work there.

In 1888 I applied to Mrs. Eddy for class instruction and was accepted. I arrived in Boston a few days before the class convened, and went to the college at 571 Columbus Avenue to see if there were any letters for me, and also to see Mr. Frye, who was Mrs. Eddy's secretary at that time. I was told that Mr. Frye was over at 385 Commonwealth Avenue, so I went over there. And then I had my first greeting from Mrs. Eddy, and it was in this wise: Just as I got there, a man drove up to the house with some provisions, and rang the bell.

We Knew Mary Baker Eddy

While he was waiting for the door to open, I walked up the steps and stood at the side of the door. When the maid opened the door, the man asked if he should bring the things in the front way or how, and while they were talking Mrs. Eddy, who was in the hall, came to the door and told him to take the things around the back way.

As he turned to go down the steps, I stepped up to the door and said, "Excuse me, but I was looking for Mr. Frye." Mrs. Eddy replied that he was not in. I then ventured to ask if this was Mrs. Eddy, and when she said it was, I told her I was Frank Gale. When I told her who I was a look came into her eyes, as she shook hands with me, that I shall never forget. I cannot describe it, but it made me feel at home. Almost the first thing she asked me was if my mother was with me. When I told her frankly that my mother was anxious to come but we did not have the funds, she said she was sorry, that it would not have been so had she known. She then expressed the hope that my mother might come to the next class.

Our Leader as Teacher and Friend

A few days later I had the blessed privilege of sitting in class, and the sunlight of Truth reflected in Mrs. Eddy's face made the cloudy days during class radiant with light. She was refinement itself. Words fail to describe her. She was so poised and dignified; and yet one felt such gentleness, humbleness, such meekness.

Mrs. Eddy asked questions of the students, going over the ground laid down in the chapter entitled "Recapitulation" in Science and Health, and of course brought in illustrations to help make it clear. There was one point that she stressed and made very positive. In order to heal quickly we must not recognize any disease in a patient, even as a belief, because we make more or less a reality of it when we do; but we should go to a patient with the feeling that he is well and we want to show him that he is well. She told us that when she had healed instantaneously she had lost sight of the personality and realized only the presence of the spiritual and perfect.

One day Mrs. Eddy allowed the class to ask

most of the questions, and at the end of the session she announced that *she* was going to do the questioning at the next lesson, and we could prepare to be *sifted*. And she kept her promise. Her keen discernment enabled her to uncover the error in thought of any student, and she never hesitated to do it, but with much love and understanding.

I shall never forget the light that shone in her face when we considered the subject of Love. As nearly as I can recall her words, she made this statement: "God is Love; to love is to express God, and as God is eternal Life, if we always loved we should always express Life, and never have a belief of death. Hate is the opposite of Love, and leads to death; therefore never hate anything."

Shortly after I returned to San Diego, my mother and I started Sunday services, which later developed into the organization of First Church of Christ, Scientist, in that city.

Whenever I read the parable of the tares and wheat, or references to this parable by Mrs. Eddy, I am reminded of a letter she wrote to me in 1891,

Our Leader as Teacher and Friend

in which she said: "You are *growing*. The Father has sealed you, and the opening of these seals must not surprise you. The character of Christ is wrought out in our lives by just such processes. The tares and wheat appear to grow together until the harvest; then the tares are *first* gathered, that is, you have seasons of seeing your errors—and afterwards by reason of this very seeing, the tares are burned, the error is destroyed. Then you see Truth plainly and the wheat is 'gathered into barns,' it becomes permanent in the understanding."

And in this same letter she added: "The healing will grow more easy and be more immediate as you realize that God, good, *is all*, and good is Love. You must gain Love, and lose the false sense called love. You must feel the Love that *never* faileth,—that perfect sense of divine power that makes healing no longer power but *grace*. Then you will have the Love that casts out fear and when fear is gone doubt is gone and your work is done. Why? because it never was *undone*."

For many years I came to Boston for the Annual

We Knew Mary Baker Eddy

Meetings, and on several occasions had interesting and instructive interviews with Mrs. Eddy.

You are all familiar with the picture of Mrs. Eddy as she stood on the balcony of her home at Pleasant View, June 29, 1903, and gave a brief address to the large gathering below (Miscellany, pp. 170, 171). I assisted in directing the people and carriages as they arrived that morning, and in the afternoon I was in the group who eagerly listened to her every word.

It is ever a source of inspiration and courage to me when I reflect on Mrs. Eddy's untiring efforts on behalf of her students and the Cause of Christian Science. Most of the letters I received from her throughout the years were in her own handwriting. And how impersonally she turned us to her works. When a new edition of Science and Health was about to be published she wrote me: "I was pleased to hear from you. Had felt that our Father was giving you line upon line and you had the best Teacher and most loving in all His ways. This abated any care of mine for you.

Our Leader as Teacher and Friend

"In reading my revised edition that is, by the way, published this week there is no special direction requisite. The general rule is to commence with the first chapter, read slowly and pause as you read to apply certain portions which meet your present need,—to thought that will carry them out in action. The book is complete in itself, it is a teacher and healer. Has 50 pages more than the old edition just past. The labor I have bestowed on it you cannot reckon, there are more signs of it than you can *see,* but not more than will be *felt.*"

May we go forward conscious of the Love which heals—that irresistible, irrepressible, fervent desire to bless, and thereby be obedient to our Leader's admonition in "Miscellaneous Writings" (pp. 206, 207): "As you journey, and betimes sigh for rest 'beside the still waters,' ponder this lesson of love. Learn its purpose; and in hope and faith, where heart meets heart reciprocally blest, drink with me the living waters of the spirit of my life-purpose,—to impress humanity with the genuine recognition of practical, operative Christian Science."

The Call to Concord
GEORGE WENDELL ADAMS

WHEN I received the unexpected call to attend the last class of our beloved Leader, Mary Baker Eddy, in Concord, New Hampshire, I had been in the active practice of Christian Science for about three years. Previously, I had received class instruction from one of Mrs. Eddy's students and had reached my decision to enter the practice while attending the Massachusetts Institute of Technology. Perhaps it should be stated here that I had become a member of The Mother Church in July, 1893, two years following my first interest in Christian Science.

The young man with whom I shared my practitioner's office also received a call from Mrs. Eddy to be in Christian Science Hall at four o'clock on Sunday afternoon, November 20, 1898. The invitations came on short notice, and there was nothing in them to indicate what was to take place. My request came by letter and my friend's came by

The Call to Concord

telegram. Both invitations were marked "confidential," so that neither of us knew at that time that the other one had been called to attend the class.

Saturday morning, November 19, the day we were to leave Boston, my friend asked me if he might borrow my suitcase. I said I was sorry but I expected to use it myself. He did not tell me why he needed it, and naturally I did not reveal to him my reason for its use. The matter was settled amicably and, later that day to our surprise, we met at the North Station in Boston and boarded the same train for Concord.

On reaching the Eagle Hotel in Concord, we saw many familiar faces. None of us knew what was to take place, and we did not discuss it because of our confidential invitations. Later we found that Mrs. Eddy's reason for observing strict secrecy about this class was to avoid the stir that might be occasioned by the many others who desired to share the great opportunity but whom she could not accommodate at that time.

Sunday morning we attended services in Christian Science Hall, which was on the site of the present edifice. Mr. Ezra M. Buswell, the First Reader, read as part of his Scriptural reading: "After these things the Lord appointed other seventy also. . . ." (Luke 10:1). This gave us our first inkling of the reason for our presence in Concord.

That afternoon each one was in his place before the appointed time. There were editors, lecturers, former doctors, lawyers, and businessmen in the class. Promptly at four o'clock our Leader entered the hall escorted by her long-time secretary, Calvin Frye. The members of the class stood up as she walked quickly and gracefully to the platform and took her place. She was vigorous and vivid and appeared much younger than her years, but there was also great meekness and holiness in her bearing. One never could forget her heavenly expression as she looked searchingly into the face of each one as he stood in response to the roll call. Well we knew that this experience would indeed impart a fresh impetus to higher spiritual attainments.

Our instruction started with God and was fol-

The Call to Concord

lowed by man. One of the outstanding things in the teaching of this class was the time given by Mrs. Eddy in her endeavor to impress upon us that there is but one God; and consequently but one full reflection,—the compound idea, man. She indicated that only as her students grasp the fundamental fact that one God could have but one full reflection, did they have the basic sense of Christian Science and the scientific starting point.

This instruction in no way conflicted with Mrs. Eddy's teaching as given in her textbook relative to individual man and ideas. Here she states in effect that Jesus' declaration, "I and my Father are one," means "one in quality, not in quantity" (Science and Health, p. 361). She further amplifies this in these words: "There is but one creator and one creation. This creation consists of the unfolding of spiritual ideas and their identities, which are embraced in the infinite Mind and forever reflected. These ideas range from the infinitesimal to infinity, and the highest ideas are the sons and daughters of God" (Science and Health, pp. 502, 503).

We Knew Mary Baker Eddy

As her wonderful teaching on this subject unfolded to us with crystal clarity, we realized more fully than ever before that: "God is indivisible. A portion of God could not enter man; neither could God's fulness be reflected by a single man, else God would be manifestly finite, lose the deific character, and become less than God. Allness is the measure of the infinite, and nothing less can express God" (Science and Health, p. 336). Nothing that Mrs. Eddy said would limit individual man from fully expressing God's qualities and the individual God-given ability to comprehend all that is real.

Our teacher's method was by questions and answers. Some of the members were asked to tell what the term God meant to them. The answers differed but all pointed to the infinite oneness of divine Principle. If one hesitated in his reply, the encouraging word was spoken, but there was no doubt but that she expected each one to speak distinctly and loud enough to be heard.

Mrs. Eddy said there were times in teaching when the deep things of Christian Science were

The Call to Concord

being considered that the mesmeric sense of too continuous seriousness must be broken. She illustrated this in her teaching of this class by telling several amusing stories.

I recall one story in particular which she used to illustrate human philosophy. She said there once was a man who had a fox. He made a hole in the door of his house and stuck the tail of the fox through it from the inside. Very shortly a crowd had gathered outside and he went out to ask why they were there. The reply was that they were trying to figure out how the fox was able to get through such a small hole. This, said Mrs. Eddy, was human philosophy, always trying to figure out things that never happened.

Mrs. Eddy clearly showed us that to heal the sick, more and more weight must be cast on the side of Spirit. Instantaneous healings were accomplished through divine Love. To live love, to manifest the very presence of Love, would heal everything. It would raise the dead.

We glimpsed as never before the true import

of the Decalogue and the Sermon on the Mount. No two days were ever filled with such practical instruction and heavenly inspiration. We had been blessed beyond words by the spiritual awakening which was ours as the result of our teacher's explanation of divine Principle. Several members of the class rose to their feet and humbly paid grateful tribute to the one whom God had "appointed to voice His Word." Indeed these loving tributes were timely expressions of our "correct sense" of divine Principle's "highest visible idea" (Science and Health, p. 560).

As the class drew to a close, we became more and more cognizant of our true heritage that "now are we the sons of God" (I John 3:2).

At parting, as we clasped Mrs. Eddy's hand and looked into her beloved face, we knew she had shared with us "God's most tender mercies" (Poems, p. 38).

An Intimate Picture of Our Leader's Final Class
SUE HARPER MIMS

ON opening the annual association meeting of her pupils held after her return from Concord, New Hampshire, Mrs. Mims read the tenth chapter of Luke, which she told us was read by the First Reader, Mr. Ezra M. Buswell, in the morning service at First Church of Christ, Scientist, in Concord. She stated that each one there felt that he had been told to read that chapter, and that the number of the class to be examined by Mrs. Eddy was indicated in the verse, "The Lord appointed other seventy also." This proved to be the case, as the number called by Mary Baker Eddy was seventy, although owing to the short notice of the call three were unable to be present.

Mrs. Mims then spoke informally, and substantially as follows:

I am just going to begin at the very beginning, and tell you everything I can possibly recall of my visit to Concord. On last Wednesday I received a letter from Mrs. Eddy, requesting me to meet her at four o'clock on the following Sunday afternoon at the Christian Science Hall in Concord. The letter stated "strictly confidential," so that no one knew where I was going but my husband, who got my ticket for me.

I was in Chattanooga Thursday night, but on Friday morning I left for Boston, arriving there at nine o'clock Saturday night. I immediately looked up the Sunday trains for Concord, and found there was but one, which left at one o'clock. I was too impatient to wait until that time; I really think I could not have slept if I had had to wait until the next day, but I found that there was a paper train which left Boston at two o'clock in the morning.

I reached Concord at five, and went right to the hotel. I did not feel at all uncomfortable about being out on the street alone at that very early hour, and did not feel tired. I rested at the hotel until time for church. The service was beautiful. As I have told you, Mr. Buswell read this beautiful

An Intimate Picture of Our Leader's Final Class

chapter from Luke. I met very many that you would all know. Mr. and Mrs. Kimball [Mr. Edward A. Kimball of Chicago] were there, and Judge and Mrs. Hanna [Judge Septimus J. Hanna, one time Editor of *The Christian Science Journal*]. There were many delightful people there, and the hotels were full.

All Concord is realizing the material good that Mrs. Eddy's residence there is bringing to the town. It has brought them much patronage in every way. They are waking up somewhat to see the spiritual gain, but they are realizing very forcibly the material benefit that Christian Science is to their beautiful little town—for it is a very beautiful little place. It is an educational point and is both active and interesting.

At four o'clock, or rather about three-thirty, everyone was seated in the little hall where First Church of Christ, Scientist, holds its meetings. On the first bench Mrs. Eddy placed those who had demonstrated a great deal from the simple study of the textbook, "Science and Health with Key to the

Scriptures." One member of the class had been healed of almost every kind of disease known to mortal mind—consumption, heart trouble, tumor, some hereditary claims—everything. She was exceedingly interesting. She was healed by reading St. John, and she had, a short time afterward, a vision of being led to the light of Truth.

There were a number of others who had had similar experiences, and our dear teacher seemed to have a peculiarly tender feeling for them. Another was a prominent lawyer and a most interesting man. When Mrs. Eddy first heard from him, she immediately wrote him not to study with anyone else but to come to her—she felt something so wonderfully receptive in his thought.

Back of that bench were those who were students of her students, and back of them were those who were her students and who were going through this class which she called a Normal class. It was, however, principally an examination with some teaching.

I would like to say something about the personnel of the class, which was very remarkable.

An Intimate Picture of Our Leader's Final Class

There were lawyers, physicians, judges, businessmen and, what was to me the most beautiful of all, several young men of twenty to twenty-five years of age, who had given up every kind of business occupation just to become Christian Scientists. There were also some very lovely young women. A physician was there, a splendid man who abandoned his profession upon coming into Christian Science, and a woman who was for twelve years the physician at Wellesley College and who gave up this work to follow Truth. Another prominent physician was also present with his wife, and many others. You would not often see a group of such refined, distinguished people collected together anywhere else in this country. All were noble and highly intellectual. But the sweetest thing to me was to see those young men—just leaving all for Christ.

One of them was in the boardinghouse where a young woman and I went, as we were to stay over for the Wednesday evening meeting. I remember we passed his door, which was standing open, and as I saw his Bible and Science and Health lying open there, it gave me such a feeling of love and tenderness to think of these young, pure thoughts going out into the world and radiating this truth.

So you can see that the personnel of the class was really extraordinary. I forgot to say that there were also two editors—young, intellectual, manly. One member of the class came from London, and another from Scotland, so that the range from Maine to California, from England and Scotland, was really marvelous.

Presently Mrs. Eddy appeared, promptly on the minute, for she is a "minute woman." Everything in her house moves in accord with Principle. I do not suppose there is a businessman in the world more methodical or more absolutely accurate than Mrs. Eddy. She said that Christian Scientists should be the most methodical people on earth because they recognize one fixed Principle. So it was promptly at four o'clock that she came into the room, and I am going to tell you just how she looked and how she was dressed. She walks very

An Intimate Picture of Our Leader's Final Class

quickly and smoothly. She is the most graceful of women. Around her neck was a little black and white ermine cape. Her beautiful white hair was in loose waves or curls around her brow. She sat in a big red-cushioned chair, which made a beautiful background for her, and when she threw back her cape it revealed a very handsome black silk dress. The skirt was of black moiré, and the waist was of white silk covered with net and heavily trimmed with jet. She wore a diamond cross given her by one of her students, and an exquisite pin presented to her by the Daughters of the American Revolution. She wore white kid gloves.

She is the very picture of refined elegance, and were I to try to describe her to you exactly, the difficulty would be to find words to express how fine she is, how delicate, how sensitive, how exquisite. The fineness of her nature shows in her very appearance, and yet with all this refinement and elegance you have never seen any human being look so meek and so holy. All of this appearance of richness one really loses sight of, as he sees this wonderful meekness and sweetness, and I think everyone who looked at her as she sat there found his eyes grow moist with love and tenderness for her.

One would be apt to think that a woman who would telegraph to every part of our country—perhaps to a judge, a lawyer, a doctor—to come and spend a few hours with her, saying that it would be a blessing to him, would be an aggressive person, a woman who felt her power and enjoyed ordering others around. Indeed, mortal mind seems to get the idea sometimes that she is stern and arbitrary. "Oh, yes," they say, "she rules them with a rod of iron; they do just what she tells them to." But if they could only see her, they would know that her motive is simply her divine love for them and for the Cause. She is obliged to know what she is; she must know that it means a blessing to come within the direct radiation of her love—but you have never in all your life seen anyone so gentle and courteous and humble and meek. You have never seen so little human will, for she knows that human will is the devil, and all that she does is done by reflecting

An Intimate Picture of Our Leader's Final Class

divine Love. And you feel this; you feel as tender as you would to a little child, and at the same time you realize the wonderful grasp and comprehensiveness of her mind. As you see more of her, you see the most delicate play of wit, and in a gentle, sweet way, the most delicate sarcasm.

She sat there and spoke to us in the most graceful way. If she tells you to do anything, she asks you to do it, in the sweetest, most pleading way you ever saw. She said how glad she was to see us all, how she had heard of us as teachers, lecturers, and workers in the Field, and had heard of our work with great satisfaction.

Then she began by doing just as we do in our class, asking each one, "What is God to you?" She pointed out that the most important thing in the world is to know God, and to know what God is. It was beautiful to watch her face as they answered. You have never seen so strange a face. She reminds me of that paragraph in Science and Health (p. 213), "Mortal mind is the harp of many strings, discoursing either discord or harmony according as the hand, which sweeps over it, is human or divine." When the replies were scientific and clear, her face was something beyond words to express. There came into it the look of one who lives in the realm of Soul. As they grasped the absolute truth, her eyes seemed to look into the realm of Spirit, and it is something one cannot describe.

One of the young men when asked this question, "What is God to you?" said, "God is Love, God is Life, Truth, Spirit. He is All-in-all; He is destruction." You should have seen her face; but she let him go on, listening to him in perfect courtesy. He was one of the young men whom she loved very dearly, and when he had finished she said gently, as I recollect it:

"Now, John, you have said that God is Life, Truth, Love, Spirit, All-in-all, and you have said that He is destruction. Will you tell me how God is destruction? Is there anything but God? What is there then to destroy?"

He answered quickly, and humbly: "Nothing, Mother, God is All, and there is nothing else. He

An Intimate Picture of Our Leader's Final Class

only destroys what seems to be unlike Himself." But the changing expression of her face during this incident impressed me very much. One could really see in her face whether error or truth was being voiced—so delicate is it, so sensitive—and it made me realize what she must have suffered when she first saw what the truth is, and then found that she must go down into the depths of error; how she cried, "Oh, let me not into the secret." She did not want to investigate the secrets of error. (See Miscellaneous Writings, pp. 222, 223.)

When she had been around the class, and everyone had answered, she said, as I remember: "You have told me wonderful things today. Now you must live up to them; you must prove them. That is what Christian Science is—it is practical. God is your Life, and there is no evil."

Then she told us something of her experience when she first saw the truth. She said the first revelation that came to her was that she could not die. She saw Life, and that it was impossible for her to die. And then she told us that three times she had raised the dead. I could not help thinking of Jesus, first raising the little maid, then the young man, and then Lazarus. She told us of one instance; she did not tell us of the others.

I think it was a long time ago. She said that she was sent for, and when she came the mother of the child was crying, "Oh, she is dead; she is dead." She put the mother out of the room, and went in and took the child in her arms. In an hour she called the mother, and the child was running across the floor to meet her.

Once she spoke substantially as follows:

"We are all learning together, and I must tell you of some of the funny things I used to do when I first saw that I had this wonderful power." (I think that her work has always been exceedingly quick.)

"My family and the friends around me saw what was done and knew that if they sent for me they would be well, but I could not make them acknowledge it. I could not make them admit what had done the healing work. One day I said, 'Oh, I *must* make them acknowledge it; I must make them

An Intimate Picture of Our Leader's Final Class

see that God does this.' Sometimes as soon as they sent for me they would be healed, before I could get there, and then they would not *know* that it was God who had done it. So one day when I was called to see a child, I was so anxious to have the power of Truth acknowledged that I said to myself, 'He *must* not get well until I get there.' Of course that was not right, for I knew I must leave it all to God, but pride had come in and I had lost my humility, and the patient was not healed. Then I saw my rebuke, and when I reached home I threw myself on the floor, put my head in my hands, and prayed that I might not be for one moment touched with the thought that I was anything or did anything; I realized that this was God's work and I reflected Him. Then the child was healed." This was the way she learned her lesson.

Then after she had finished speaking, her students arose and gave their experiences. Judge Hanna said that he had once been the instrument through which death had been destroyed. I do not think he said that the patient had really passed on but

that it w̶   ̶e said that he
went int̶o   ̶realization of
Life that̶   ̶.

The young man, of whom I have previously spoken, arose to speak but was so overcome with emotion that he had to sit down. It was quite a few moments before he could proceed. He said that Christian Science had come to him in a marvelous burst of light. Three times he had a vision of wonderful, intense light, in which he was simply bathed, a light beyond the brightness of the sun or any light that is known. I have never seen anything like her face when he told of it. It simply quivered. Her look was wonderful as she said, as I recall it: "Yes, I felt it when you wrote to me, and you are nearer to me in the resurrection thought than anyone I ever touched. That is the reason I told you not to go to anyone else to be taught, but to come to me."

There were a number of other interesting experiences. One lady said that once or twice a brilliant light had flooded her book as she was reading.

Mrs. Eddy, when the class was over, said she

An Intimate Picture of Our Leader's Final Class

had not known before how many days she would teach, but this class had been so satisfactory that she would have only one more session, which would be the next day. She said she would make no charge for this class. "When first establishing this Cause," I recall her saying, "I needed money, but I have now learned that God is with me, that He gives me everything, and I cannot lack." A little later she added, as I recollect, "When you stand before a mirror and look at your reflection, it is the same as the original. Now you are God's reflection. If His hands are full, your hands are full, if you image Him. You cannot know lack. I have learned now that He does give us everything."

Then she asked us questions. One was, "What is the best way to do instantaneous healing?" Many arose. Some said, "Realize the ever-presence of good;" others, "Deny the claims of evil." There were many answers, but when they had finished, she said, as I remember: "I will tell you the way to do it. It is to love! Just live love—be it—love, love, love. Do not know anything but Love. Be all love.

We Knew Mary Baker Eddy

There is nothing else. That will do the work. It will heal everything; it will raise the dead. *Be* nothing but love."

Then there came up what was, to me, the most interesting question in the whole class. Someone said, "But, Mother, are we not to discriminate between good and evil?" She answered substantially as follows: "Ah, now you have asked me what is to me the hardest thing in Christian Science! Yes, you must see and denounce evil. The Bible tells us that Jesus was God's chosen because he loved righteousness, but the Bible does not stop there. It says, 'and hated iniquity'! So often have I longed to see and know only Love—only the good—but I have not dared. I *must* uncover and rebuke and *hate* iniquity."

This was very valuable to us all. To her this is the greatest struggle of all, the hardest thing in Science, but when one *loves* righteousness, one *hates* iniquity.

Then she spoke of the absurdity of the literal translation of the Bible. Everything in the Bible, she told us, has its spiritual interpretation, though

An Intimate Picture of Our Leader's Final Class

many see only the literal meaning. And she added the following humorous story: "Once there was a man who engaged another man to hoe in his field for him. In the middle of the day the workman came to the employer and said, 'I want to go and get some water for I am thirsty.' 'No, you cannot go,' said the employer. 'Why when I have been working hard and am thirsty,' said the man, 'can I not go and get some water?' 'Because it is contrary to the Bible,' was the reply. 'How is that?' asked the other. 'Why, the Bible says, "Ho, every one that thirsteth"!' "

Once in the course of the examination she said substantially:

"My dear ones, I would love it very much—I would feel it a great favor—if you would translate for me into the new tongue some passages from the Bible. Who will do this for me?" Her tone was so gentle and soft and pleading. A splendid, stalwart boy arose and, as no one else seemed to, I stood up. Then someone said: "Mother, we will all do it; we all want to do it." So she found the twenty-fourth chapter of Luke (you can see how she dwells in the resurrection thought) and asked the young man to translate the first verse spiritually for her. It was, "Now upon the first day of the week, very early in the morning, they came unto the sepulchre, bringing the spices which they had prepared, and certain others with them."

He began to explain it, stumbling along like a big schoolboy: "Well, Mother, you know they were women, and women have the highest idea of God." Here, as I remember, she said softly, "I don't know about that." "They saw a new idea of God," he continued, "and they brought spices, which were their loving thoughts."

When he had finished, she called me and made me come and sit upon the platform by her side, saying she wanted them all to see me. Then she asked me to translate the second verse. I did not remember it, but when she handed me the Bible I found it was, "And they found the stone rolled away from the sepulchre."

"The stone," I said, "was the concentrated

An Intimate Picture of Our Leader's Final Class

human belief that life was limited, and they saw that Life had rolled it away and that man was immortal—that he was never born and never dies." I closed by saying, "They saw what our beloved mother has through Science and Health enabled us to see. Through the book we have seen all that they saw and more, and we owe it all to her, to this beloved one who is God's messenger today."

When I had given her back the book and gone to my seat, she said in effect:

"You have given a very beautiful exegesis of the text, but I have one objection—I may say I have one fault to find—it was not necessary to mention me."

Then I wish you could have seen that class. One arose with wet eyes and said, "Mother, how could we forget you?" Judge Hanna got up, and it was one of the most heart-rending things I ever heard in my life, as he said:

"Mother, let me tell you this. Sometimes all the machinations of evil that are conceivable to the human mind seem to be hurled at us, and sometimes for days the world seems black. Every argument that the ingenuity of evil can suggest whispers, trying to hide your mission, and the light returns only when we see you as you are—the revelator of this Truth."

Others spoke on the same line. It was the most beautiful thing, and you see that had to be brought out. She had to be acknowledged, and yet while they were speaking you have never seen such humility, such self-effacement, in your life. And then she said, according to my recollection: "My dear children, if you had not seen it, I should have had to teach you this. I could not have avoided telling you that when my students become blinded to me as the one through whom Truth has come in this age, they miss the path. I would have had to tell you."

The tears of joy were on her face, and that strange, wonderful look that perhaps no mortal face ever had, since Jesus and Paul. Perhaps no face was ever more tender. It was filled with meekness and humility, yet the responsibility was hers of making us know that when we do not see her as she is, we lose the way.

An Intimate Picture of Our Leader's Final Class

There is not a day of my life that I do not declare at least once, often twice, that malicious animal magnetism cannot blind me to her. We must fix our gaze on Principle, think of God, and yet we must recognize who she is.

At the close of the class she said in effect, "I cannot tell you the joy this class is to me. I am so pleased and satisfied. I feel the years roll off me!" What a wonderful thing to say!

There are no words to tell what the radiation of love, just from her presence, is. She gave us a beautiful interpretation of what it means to "run, and not be weary; . . . walk, and not faint" (Isaiah 40:31). She takes it right into metaphysics. When we are working to overcome error, or are handling a case that does not seem to yield, we shall not be discouraged or wearied by the work, nor can there be any reaction. We shall go on without suffering or being weary, even though the demonstration is slow.

She told us one thing that we should all remember. She said, as I recall, "Now I want you to speak distinctly. When you speak distinctly it shows your mental quality. Speak as if you had something that you wanted the world to hear. Speak loud and strong and distinctly." Her own voice is very clear.

Of our source of supply she said in substance, "It is like a scale. On one side is the infinite good —that is the side of Spirit. Everything we put in the scale of Spirit is in the scale of infinity, but materiality means limitation, and everything we put in the side of matter, we put in the scale of limitation."

"In the human," I recall her adding, "it is good for us to think of God as our Father and Mother, with us every moment, giving us everything, clothing us, feeding us, giving us everything good and beautiful, caring for our human bodies. But in metaphysics man is the image of God. Man never was a child to grow. In metaphysics, man reflects all that God is. God is the trinity, Life, Truth, and Love; man is the idea of Life, Truth, and Love. Man is just as old as God, and he reflects all that

An Intimate Picture of Our Leader's Final Class

God is and all that God has. We must live in the thought of His ever-present infinite Life and Love."

Of making her gifts, she said in effect: "I want no material gifts. I want spiritual gifts. I would rather have one outstanding healing than all the gifts on earth. These are the gifts I want—your own spiritual growth, your own demonstrations."

I think now that I have told you all. What I wanted to make you see was her wonderful meekness, humility, gentleness, courtesy, and love. I do not think anyone in this room will ever adore the personality of Mrs. Eddy, but you will love her and reverence her as the highest manifestation of Love that is in the world, or that has been for eighteen hundred years, as the Leader of the greatest movement that ever was, the movement that is establishing the kingdom of God on earth; as the one through whom God is being enthroned in the hearts of humanity. I was so glad that I could say what God is, in the exact words of the book.

I did not have a private talk with Mrs. Eddy. At the close of the class she shook hands with us all.

An Interview with Mary Baker Eddy, and Other Memories

MARY STEWART

IT should be understood that, when I quote Mrs. Eddy in the address which I am about to give, the wording is as I vividly recall it, and is substantially correct.

I wish that you all, especially those of you who never saw our Leader, Mary Baker Eddy, or heard her speak, might have been with me one day in January, 1901, as I waited a few moments for her in her library at Pleasant View, and felt, before seeing her, the loving presence I was invited to enter. She came with a light step and a pleasant greeting. I saw again this beautiful, gentle woman —daintily gowned, ready to go for her usual drive after my call. Her hair was silvery white, soft, and becomingly dressed; her face unwrinkled and lovely in coloring; her expression vivacious and constantly changing with her thoughts; her eyes large, deep and blue, sometimes laughing, sometimes tender,

An Interview with Mary Baker Eddy

sometimes sad for a moment as she spoke of a lawsuit, to which she was having to give much time, and of some conditions in the Field. Her voice was colorful, firm, refined, and she talked with her lips, her eyes, her hands, and from her heart.

Our Leader exemplified her words in *Christian Science Series* (Vol. I, No. 1). There she speaks of the effect of accumulative years and says, "The added wisdom of age and experience is strength, not weakness, and we should understand this, expect it, and know that it is so, then it would appear."

I was in Concord in response to a telegram to come at once. I found five other Scientists at Christian Science Hall, and learned that we were called to do some preliminary work toward winning a suit which had been brought against Mrs. Eddy and some of the officers of The Mother Church. Living at a greater distance than the others, I arrived a day later. They had had an interview with our Leader that afternoon, but in the evening, with her unfailing graciousness, she sent one of her secretaries with a message to me and an invitation to call on her the next day. The message she sent was this: "Tell her that her prompt obedience to the call will ensure to her life, health, and heaven." This interview seemed to me a foretaste of heaven.

When Mrs. Eddy entered the room that day, she seated herself in a chair close to mine and at once asked, "What did So-and-so [the secretary] say to you last evening?" I replied, "Mother, he said that he had discovered self-justification in himself." With the merriest laugh she said, "Oh, he did not discover it, I did!" Then followed the most precious three quarters of an hour I have ever experienced except in her class.

She talked earnestly of the welfare of the Cause and of the Field; of how error tried to separate some of her oldest students from the church; of her last class and of teaching in general; and of some of her early healings.

She told of a healing of heart disease, and of cancer, instantaneously, and emphasized the neces-

An Interview with Mary Baker Eddy

sity for giving much time and consecration to the work of healing, adding, "I cannot help healing." It was her great love and spirituality which made healing as natural to her as it was to Jesus. In class she had taught us that it is "Love" that heals the dying.

Continuing to talk about Christian Science healing she said: "The worst evil is to go to a bed of sickness and say: God is All. God is Love. You are not sick." She spoke with scorn of such statements made coldly and superficially, and indicated that that sort of practice sometimes amounted to neglect of a case and brought criticism from physicians, saying: "If I were a physician I would have made the same criticisms, and they would have been just. How I decry such practice!" Then with a light in her eyes and filled with the power of Spirit she said, "Mother would say, Arise and walk!" Like Jesus, our Leader healed quickly and permanently, not fearing to use the sword of the Spirit to separate evil from person.

Mrs. Eddy related some of the efforts of evil

against her, saying that there were those who were working to separate churches, break up the ranks; "to separate from me," she said, "to break up my household." As she said this her face was illumined with the Christ-spirit—her look and attitude declaring her dominion. The threats of evil and their boastfulness seemed so absurd, impossible, and impudent that I laughed. Instantly she said: "If you take it that way, perhaps you could stand. Yes, you can—and having done all, stand." This recalls her statement in "Unity of Good" (p. 17), "A lie has only one chance of successful deception, —to be accounted true."

As we stood together a moment before she went for her drive, she remarked, "I feel that I have known you always." That exactly expressed what I had been feeling—so gracious was she in her ability to make one feel at home. We had all felt this unity with her in class.

During the time the group of Scientists were working together it was evident that Mrs. Eddy was constantly listening for God's direction. She

An Interview with Mary Baker Eddy

sent us instructions about how to work, then told us to wait; then again came definite instruction. Ever did she exemplify her words in "Miscellaneous Writings" (Pref., p. xii), "With armor on, I continue the march, command and countermand." When that part of the work for which this group had been called was accomplished, she directed us to return to our homes. She wrote: "I deeply thank you for your Christlikeness in coming and going at the word. Our Master did just this. I have done it for thirty years."

Much of the spirit and letter of our Leader's last class have been given by other students in published articles, such as her statement of the Trinity; her teaching of God as Father, Mother, Shepherd, and other never-to-be-forgotten instruction. There was much to encourage and comfort the younger members of the class. She said: "I will lift you into the understanding." "All is God's; everything belongs to Him. You reflect it all." "I have made you learners."

She told us that in her early experience in

Christian Science her work was so quick that people who sent for her were healed before she reached their homes, and often did not acknowledge that Christian Science had anything to do with their recovery.

In this class, through our teacher's pure love and spirituality, I caught an illuminating sense of *reflection*. Where there is reflection there is light. She handled animal magnetism from the standpoint of the allness of Spirit, reducing it to nothingness through the ever-present Christ-power.

Mrs. Eddy asked nothing for herself personally. As we understand her better, we can give more to the Cause for which she laid down all. Only as we recognize the revelator can we understand and obey the revelation. As the prophecies of Jesus and of John were fulfilled through her, so must we, her followers, do our part in fulfilling her prediction for the twentieth century (Pulpit and Press, p. 22): "Christ will give to Christianity his new name, and Christendom will be classified as Christian Scientists."

"With sandals on and staff in hand"
CLARA KNOX MC KEE

IT is a great privilege to write about our dear Leader, Mary Baker Eddy, whom I had the opportunity of knowing personally and serving at Pleasant View during one of the greatest trials of her life. I was called to Pleasant View in August, 1906. Several months later there was filed in the New Hampshire Court the so-called "Next Friends" suit which was brought against her, to deprive her of the management of her property. This trial lasted until August 21, 1907, when the so-called "Next Friends" and their attorneys were forced to admit that they could not sustain any of the charges in their petition, and thereupon filed a motion for dismissal of the suit.

If you could have known our Leader at that time, you would have realized that she was in the arms of divine Love. While doing everything necessary to defend herself and her publications, she went right on with her daily duties and her writing, thus magnificently fulfilling her own words, "As of old, I stand with sandals on and staff in hand, waiting for the watchword and the revelation of what, how, whither" (Miscellaneous Writings, p. 158).

At that time, she was revising "Science and Health with Key to the Scriptures." She had a copy of the three-dollar edition taken apart in sections; this was placed right side up in the left-hand side of her desk drawer. She would take off one section at a time and go through it. Then that one was placed upside down in the right-hand side of the drawer. When she had finished going over every page of the entire book, it was in perfect order.

In "Miscellaneous Writings" (p. 311) our Leader says, "The works I have written on Christian Science contain absolute Truth, and my necessity was to tell it; . . . I was a scribe under orders; . . ." Again in "The First Church of Christ, Scientist, and Miscellany" (p. 251), she writes, "Adhere to the teachings of the Bible, Science and Health, and our Manual, and you will obey the law and

"*With sandals on and staff in hand*"

gospel. Have one God and you will have no devil."

The Christian Science Journal was our first periodical, edited and published by Mrs. Eddy. Mrs. Eddy commented about the *Journal* as follows (Miscellaneous Writings, p. 4): "At this date, 1883, a newspaper edited and published by the Christian Scientists has become a necessity. . . . Further enlightenment is necessary for the age, and a periodical devoted to this work seems alone adequate to meet the requirement." In the same article she adds (p. 7), "Looking over the newspapers of the day, one naturally reflects that it is dangerous to live, so loaded with disease seems the very air. . . . A periodical of our own will counteract to some extent this public nuisance; for through our paper, at the price at which we shall issue it, we shall be able to reach many homes with healing, purifying thought." Thus in April, 1883, she started the *Journal*. The first volume consisted of six numbers; the second volume of ten. The third volume was the first which corresponded in size to its present form. Thus from small beginnings sprang the *Journal* which now goes to all parts of the world.

Like the *Journal*, the *Christian Science Sentinel* began in Mrs. Eddy's thought as a newspaper. In a letter to Mr. William P. McKenzie, Trustee, dated August 20, 1898, she wrote, "The dignity of our cause and the good of the students demand of us to publish a weekly newspaper" (Historical Sketches, p. 127). It was first published as *The Christian Science Weekly*, September 1, 1898. Christian Scientists were very grateful for this little paper coming every week.

In a letter to Judge Hanna, she wrote, "Sentinel is the proper title for our Weekly. . . . Also let me prophesy 'Sentinel' and the motto with it describes the future of this newspaper. It will take that place and must *fill it* when numerous periodicals of our denomination are extant" (Historical Sketches, p. 127).

The first issue of the *Sentinel* under its new name appeared January 26, 1899, with its new motto, "What I say unto you I say unto all, WATCH."

"With sandals on and staff in hand"

So we see that the words "Sentinel" and "watch" indicate the permanent position of this periodical.

Several months later Mrs. Eddy made a By-Law in regard to our periodicals which reads: "It shall be the privilege and duty of every member, who can afford it, to subscribe for the periodicals which are the organs of this Church; and it shall be the duty of the Directors to see that these periodicals are ably edited and kept abreast of the times" (Church Manual, p. 44).

Mrs. Eddy depended radically on divine guidance. When she felt sure that the divine Mind had spoken to her, she did not hesitate to act. Her attitude was that she had to obey God. This she did, sometimes even before she knew the reason for doing so. One instance of this occurred during the trial already referred to. As we are told in the book, "Historical Sketches," by Judge Clifford P. Smith (p. 130), Mrs. Eddy "called a consultation of her lawyers, and found that they agreed to take a certain position which she regarded as unwise. A full discussion made no change. After they left her, she sent for Mr. Elder, told him that they were wrong, and obtained his promise that he would ask the other lawyers to reconsider the question." They did so, with the result "that they reversed their decision, followed the lines insisted upon by Mrs. Eddy, and during the trial it became indubitably clear that she had been right."

During my stay at Pleasant View, Mrs. Eddy often called her lawyers for interviews. Many reporters sought interviews, some of which were granted.

Mr. William E. Curtis of the *Chicago Record-Herald*, after an interview, made this remark, "I have never seen a woman eighty-six years of age with greater physical or mental vigor" (Historical Sketches, p. 131).

Mr. Arthur Brisbane of the *New York Evening Journal* and the *Cosmopolitan Magazine* said, "It is quite certain that nobody could see this beautiful and venerable woman and ever again speak of her except in terms of affectionate reverence and sympathy." I had the privilege of meeting

"With sandals on and staff in hand"

these eminent editors and writers at Pleasant View.

During this trial, it seemed that every phase of evil presented itself to be met and destroyed. One day Mrs. Eddy called her students into her study and pointed to a very black cloud, shaped like a cornucopia, coming toward the house in direct line with her front study window. She asked each one to go to a window and face it, and to realize that there were no destructive elements in God's creation. Although appearing to whirl straight toward Pleasant View, a mile or so away the cyclone changed its course and went around Concord into the mountains, doing very little damage.

Mrs. Eddy had a keen, delightful sense of humor. One day while I was busy in her room, she was reading a letter; looking up, she called me and said in substance, "How do they demonstrate money and furniture?" I replied, "I do not know, I was not taught that." Then, as I recall, she said, "Thank God you were not. We demonstrate Life, Truth, and Love, and *they* give us our supplies; we do not *demonstrate* material things."

We Knew Mary Baker Eddy

Mrs. Eddy was very fond of little children. One day she told me of a little boy and a little girl who came each May Day to hang a basket of arbutus on her door. She asked me to watch for them and bring them in to see her. I did so, and much to their embarrassment I took them up to her room. She talked lovingly to them about their school and Sunday School, and thanked them for the flowers and the love that prompted their gift. After they were gone, she asked Mr. Frye to get them each a little gold ring next time he went to Concord.

There is a sweet picture of Mrs. Eddy as the Founder, Discoverer, and Leader of Christian Science which I have retained in memory.

I see her in the early morning, dressed, ready for the day, seated in her study beside her writing desk, in the bay window, with her Bible and the textbook in her lap. Calm, serene, silently communing with divine Love, as evidenced by the faraway look in her eyes, she seemed to be looking into reality. There she was, waiting for the workers

"With sandals on and staff in hand"

whom she had just called in for the morning talk. When all were gathered before her, she would open her Bible at random and read the first thing her eyes fell upon. Then she would give the spiritual interpretation of it, which flowed from her lips as freely as if she had written it out.

This was her bread from heaven, her inspiration and revelation, the manna for the day, which she shared with the members of her household. It was clear that because of her spirituality she was the revelator of Christian Science, its Discoverer, Founder, and Leader.

The religion which Mrs. Eddy founded is her great legacy to humanity by which mankind may choose the good and reject the evil. To reject the evil and *accept* the good is the operation or working order of Christian Science itself. Mrs. Eddy's gift to us is the revelation of the truth of being. The organization which she founded makes available to all mankind the life-giving waters of Truth. In Revelation we read, "And the Spirit and the bride say, Come. . . . And let him that is athirst come.

And whosoever will, let him take the water of life freely."

The Mother Church, The First Church of Christ, Scientist, in Boston, Massachusetts, together with The Christian Science Publishing Society, and the periodicals it publishes, were founded and established by our Leader. They are safeguarded by the Manual of The Mother Church which, through the inspired provisions of its By-Laws, protects and preserves the Christian Science movement.

The law of true Christianity is manifest in the activities of The Mother Church. Moses gave us the moral law. Elias exemplified prophecy. Christ Jesus demonstrated the divine law in the destruction of sin, disease, and death. Mrs. Eddy gave us the Science of Christianity which forever reveals to all mankind the practical application of the divine law in everyday experience. The Mother Church, the government and laws of which are God-derived, enables each member who faithfully adheres to its teachings to be properly self-governed, for he demonstrates that God alone governs him.

"With sandals on and staff in hand"

Of the ideal woman it is said in Proverbs 31:26: "She openeth her mouth with wisdom; and in her tongue is the law of kindness." This certainly is descriptive of our beloved Leader and friend, Mary Baker Eddy. In her Message to The Mother Church in 1902 (p. 4) she said, "Competition in commerce, deceit in councils, dishonor in nations, dishonesty in trusts, begin with 'Who shall be greatest?' I again repeat, Follow your Leader, only so far as she follows Christ."

We know she was a faithful follower of the Christ. May her wonderful example continue to guide and illuminate our lives!

INDEX

INDEX

A

Abraham, 4
Animal magnetism, handled, 10, 11, 55, 64

B

Bible, 20, 37, 40, 66, 72, 73; quoted, 3, 4, 6, 11, 12, 14, 16, 30, 34, 55, 75; spiritually interpreted, 50-53
Blackman, C. Lulu, first healing in Christian Science, 1, 2; first patient, 9-11, letter to Mrs. Eddy, 3
Boston, Mass., 9, 15, 17, 21, 25, 29, 36
Brisbane, Arthur, 70
Buswell, Ezra M., 30, 35, 36
By-Laws, 69, 74 *See also* Manual

C

Chicago, Ill., 1, 2, 37
Chicago Record-Herald, 70
Christ Jesus, 11, 18, 46, 50, 64, 74
Christian Science, and Christianity, 64
  healings in, 1, 2, 20, 21, 63, 64; instantaneous, 23, 25, 33, 47-49; specific cases: consumption, 38; erysipelas, 9, 10; heart trouble, 38; hereditary disease, 38; raising the dead, 33; tumor, 38
  movement, Mrs. Eddy's care over, 26, 60; protected by the Manual, 74
  must be proved practical, 45, 61, 74
  scientific starting point, 31
  unity in, 20
Christian Science Hall, Concord, N. H., 28-30, 36, 37, 59; Sunday services, 29, 30, 36
Christian Science Journal, The, 37, 67, 68
Christian Science periodicals, 69, 74 *See also Christian Science Journal, The, Christian Science Sentinel, Christian Science Weekly, The*
Christian Science practitioners, early, 21, 28
Christian Science Publishing Society, The, 74
Christian Science Sentinel, 68, 69
Christian Science Series, 59
Christian Science Weekly, The, 68
Christianity and Christian Science, 64
Class instruction, 20, 22, 23, 28
Class of 1885, 1-19; composition of, 5, 6
Concord, N. H., 17, 29, 35, 36, 59, 71, 72; benefits from Mrs. Eddy's residence, 37
Cosmopolitan Magazine, 70
Curtis, William E., 70

D

Daughters of the American Revolution, 41
Decalogue, 34

[79]

Index

E

Eagle Hotel, Concord, N. H., 29
Eddy, Mary Baker, as Discoverer, 45, 46, 73
  as Founder, 67–69, 73, 74
  as healer, early cases: heart disease and cancer, 60; raised the dead, 46; instantaneous cures, 46, 60, 61; learned through early mistakes, 46, 47; naturalness of, 61; work not always acknowledged, 46, 47, 64
  as Leader, 73; addressed followers at Pleasant View, 26; constantly turned to God for guidance, 62, 63, 69; interviews with followers, 21, 22, 26, 58–64, 70; qualities, 8, 40, 42, 54, 57, 62; shunned personal adulation, 11, 26, 53, 54, 57, 64, 75; stressed need for unity, 20
  as preacher, exposition of Psalm 91, 15
  as revelator of Truth, 3, 4, 12, 64, 73
  as teacher, 5, 21, 22; of class of 1885, 1–19; counseled students to speak up, 32, 56; demanded healing works, 8, 9, 61; explained the Trinity, 63; gave instructions on Love, 24, 25; on prayer, 6, 7; on the question of evil, 12, 14; on source of supply, 49, 56; handled animal magnetism, 64; of last class (a Normal class), 28–57, 60, 63; Biblical interpretations, 50–53; confidential invitations, 29, 36; corrected incorrect answer, 44, 45; demanded practical proofs, 45; extraordinary personnel, 30, 37–40, 42, 43, 48, 63; final greetings, 34, 55, 57; instructions on instantaneous healings, 49, 50, 55; instructions on need to uncover and rebuke evil, 50; instructions on relations of God and man, 30–32, 43, 44, 56, 57; no fee charged, 49; students' reports, 47, 48; relations with students, 5, 6, 26, 62; taught: both letter and spirit, 8, 9, how to heal quickly, 23, 25, importance of adhering to Bible, *Science and Health*, and the Manual, 66, that Love heals the dying, 61, the true concept of God, 10, 63, the value of humor, 33; through *Science and Health*, 2, 31; tolerated no notes, 7, 8; uncovered error in students, 24; used question and answer method, 23, 24, 32; warned of need to protect one's work, 16
  as writer of *Science and Health*, 2, 3, 27, 66
balcony portait, 26
benefits Concord, N. H., 37
daily drive, 17, 62
descriptions of, 4, 5, 9, 11, 13–15, 18, 23, 30, 40–42, 58, 59, 70, 72, 73
desired only spiritual gifts from followers, 57
financial resources, 49

[80]

Index

Eddy, Mary Baker (cont.)
  fondness for children, 72
  fulfilled prophecy, 64
  gave advice on reading the textbook, 27
  gifts from students, 41; from the DAR, 41
  homes, 21, 58
  household, 65, 70–73
  interpreted Biblical passages, 24, 25, 55, 72, 73
  letters to individual followers, 3, 4, 24–27, 60, 68
  life purpose, 27
  opposition to, 5, 6, 13, 14, 61, 62, 65, 66; lawsuits, 59, 65, 69, 70
  quotations (unpublished), 16, 24, 49, 50, 54–56, 71
  recognition of, 18, 53–55
  resisted investigation of error, 45
  reversed evidence of destructive elements, 71
  scorned superficial statements, 61
  shunned use of human will, 42, 43
  students, disloyal, 60; early, 2, 28
  studied *Science and Health*, 72
  wit, 33, 51, 71
Elder, Mr. (Samuel J.), 70
Elias, 74

F

First Church of Christ, Scientist, and Miscellany, The, by Mrs. Eddy, quoted, 20, 26, 66
First Church of Christ, Scientist, Concord, N. H., 35, 37
First Church of Christ, Scientist, in Boston, Massachusetts, The *See* Mother Church, The
First Church of Christ, Scientist, San Diego, Calif., 24
Frye, Calvin, 21, 22, 30, 72

G

Gale, Frank Walter, letters from Mrs. Eddy, 26, 27; meetings with Mrs. Eddy, 21, 22, 26
God, as preeminent subject of Mrs. Eddy's teaching, 30–32, 43, 56

H

Hanna, Judge and Mrs. Septimus J., 37, 47, 48, 53, 54, 68
Healings *See* Christian Science, healings in
Herod thought, 16
Historical Sketches, by Clifford P. Smith, 68–70
Human philosophy, described by Mrs. Eddy, 33

J

Jesus *See* Christ Jesus
John, St., 64

K

Kimball, Mr. and Mrs. Edward A., 37

L

Last class *See* Eddy, Mary Baker, as teacher of last class
Law, true Christian, 74
Lazarus, 46
London, England, 40
Lord's Prayer, 6, 7

Index

Love, as subject of Mrs. Eddy's teaching, 12, 24

M

Man, as important subject of Mrs. Eddy's teaching, 31, 32, 56
Man and the fox, Mrs. Eddy's story of, 33
Manual, 20, 66, 69, 74
Massachusetts Institute of Technology, 28
Massachusetts Metaphysical College, 21
McKenzie, William P., 68
Mesmerism, broken by humor, 33
Message to The Mother Church for 1902, by Mrs. Eddy, quoted, 75
Metaphysical healing, 1
Miscellaneous Writings, by Mrs. Eddy, quoted, 13, 18, 27, 45, 63, 66, 67
Moses, 74
Mother Church, The, 28, 74; officers of, 59

N

Nebraska, 1
New Hampshire, 65
New York Evening Journal, 70
"Next Friends" suit, 65, 69, 70
Normal class *See* Eddy, Mary Baker, as teacher of last class

P

Pleasant View (Mrs. Eddy's home), 17, 26, 58, 65, 70, 71; address by Mrs. Eddy to followers in 1903, 26
Poems, by Mrs. Eddy, 34
Prayer, Christian Science teaching on, 6, 7

Psalm 91, 15
Pulpit and Press, by Mrs. Eddy, quoted, 64

R

"Recapitulation," (chapter in *Science and Health*), 23
Reflection, its meaning made clear, 64
Resurrection, spiritually interpreted, 52, 53
Revelation, book of, 73, 74

S

San Diego, Calif., 21, 24
San Francisco, Calif., 21
Science and Health with Key to the Scriptures, by Mrs. Eddy, 2, 20, 21, 23, 40, 53, 72; as teacher, 27, 31, 37, 38, 66; Mrs. Eddy's advice on how to read, 27; quoted, 10, 12, 14, 15, 18, 31, 32, 34, 43, 44; revised, 26, 27, 66
Scotland, 40
Self-government, 74
Sermon on the Mount, 34
Smith, Clifford P., 69

T

Tares and wheat, Mrs. Eddy's exposition of parable, 24, 25
Ten Commandments, 34
Trinity, the, 63

U

Unity of Good, by Mrs. Eddy, quoted, 11, 62

W

Wellesley College, 39

[82]